I0820843

INSIDE THE NFL

JACKSONVILLE JAGUARS

by Charlie Beattie

An imprint of Abdo Publishing
abdobooks.com

ABDOBOOKS.COM

Published by Abdo Publishing, a division of ABDO, PO Box 398166, Minneapolis, Minnesota 55439.

Printed in China.
052025
092025

Cover Photos: Courtney Culbreath/Getty Images Sport/Getty Images (Trevor Lawrence); George Gojkovich/Getty Images Sport/Getty Images (Fred Taylor)
Interior Photos: David Rosenblum/Icon Sportswire/Getty Images, 4–5, 8, 58; Perry Knotts/Getty Images Sport/Getty Images, 6, 57; Douglas P. DeFelice/Getty Images Sport/Getty Images, 7, 9; Abdo Publishing, 10–11; Al Messerschmidt/Getty Images Sport/Getty Images, 12–13, 42 (bottom); Al Messerschmidt Archive/AP Images, 14–15; Chris Wilkins/AFP/Getty Images, 16; Brian Bahr/AFP/Getty Images, 17, 60 (bottom left); David Durochik/AP Images, 18; David J. Phillip/AP Images, 19, 52; Jamie Squire/Allsport/Getty Images Sport/Getty Images, 20; David Maxwell/AFP/Getty Images, 21; Andy Lyons/Allsport/Getty Images Sport/Getty Images, 22–23; Paul K. Buck/AFP/Getty Images, 24–25; Scott Halleran/Allsport/Getty Images Sport/Getty Images, 26; Michael S. Green/AP Images, 27; George Gojkovich/Getty Images Sport/Getty Images, 28, 30, 42 (top), 60 (top); Andy Lyons/Getty Images Sport/Getty Images, 29, 38; Don Frazier/AP Images, 31; Robert Sullivan/AFP/Getty Images, 32; Roberto Schmidt/AFP/Getty Images, 33; Peter Muhly/AFP/Getty Images, 35, 60 (bottom right); Michael J. Minardi/Getty Images Sport/Getty Images, 36–37; David Stluka/AP Images, 39; Paul Spinelli/AP Images, 40; Jim McIsaac/Getty Images Sport/Getty Images, 41; Keith Srakocic/AP Images, 43, 61 (top left); Rob Tringali/SportsChrome/Getty Images, 44; Felix Mizioznikov/Shutterstock Images, 45; Grant Halverson/Getty Images Sport/Getty Images, 46–47; LM Otero/AP Images, 48, 61 (bottom); Matt Patterson/AP Images, 49; Sam Greenwood/Getty Images Sport/Getty Images, 50 (top); Leslie Plaza Johnson/Icon Sportswire/Getty Images, 50 (bottom), 63; Maddie Meyer/Getty Images Sport/Getty Images, 51, 61 (top right); Don Juan Moore/Getty Images Sport/Getty Images, 53; Phelan M. Ebenhack/AP Images, 54; Shutterstock Images, 56

Editor: Rebecca Higgins
Series Designer: Laura Graphenteen
Production Designer: Laura Kuchar

Library of Congress Control Number: 2024948502

Publisher's Cataloging-in-Publication Data Publishers Info

Names: Beattie, Charlie, author.
Title: Jacksonville Jaguars / by Charlie Beattie
Description: Minneapolis, Minnesota: Abdo Publishing, 2026 | Series: Inside the NFL | Includes online resources and index.
Identifiers: ISBN 9781098296766 (lib. bdg.) | ISBN 9798384919285 (ebook)
Subjects: LCSH: Jacksonville Jaguars (Football team)--Juvenile literature. | National Football League--Juvenile literature. | Football teams--Juvenile literature. | American football--Juvenile literature.
Classification: DDC 796.33264--dc23

CONTENTS

Jacksonville Jaguars wide receiver Christian Kirk scores a touchdown against the Los Angeles Chargers.

CHAPTER 1

A CLUTCH KICK

THE PRESSURE WAS HIGH AS JACKSONVILLE JAGUARS KICKER RILEY Patterson stepped onto the field. Only three seconds remained in the game on January 14, 2023. Jacksonville was facing the Los Angeles Chargers in the American Football Conference (AFC) wild-card playoff game. Jacksonville trailed 30–28. Patterson's kick would decide whether his Jaguars continued in the postseason or if their season would end there.

Jacksonville seemed outmatched earlier in the game. Los Angeles led 27–0 late in the second quarter. Just before halftime, Jaguars quarterback Trevor Lawrence threw a touchdown pass. But the team still trailed by 20 points.

When Jacksonville returned for the second half, they had flipped a switch. Lawrence tossed three more touchdowns to bring his team to within two points. Then, with only 1:28 remaining in the game, Jaguars rookie running back Travis Etienne took the handoff on fourth-and-one from the Chargers' 41-yard line and sprinted to the right for a 25-yard gain. The play put the Jags in field-goal position. Jacksonville ran one more play, then ran the clock down to three seconds. The team's fate depended on Patterson.

TOPSY-TURVY

The up-and-down wild-card playoff game against the Chargers was a fitting metaphor for the Jaguars. Jacksonville joined the National Football League (NFL) in 1995. Entering the 2022 season, Jacksonville had made the playoffs only once in the previous 14 seasons. The team had won only four games and lost 29 in the past two years. But the Jaguars had budding

Quarterback Trevor Lawrence reacts during a game against the Houston Texans in October 2022.

young star quarterback Lawrence. Fans hoped 2022 would be a winning year.

The excitement around Jacksonville was buoyed by a 2–1 start. But Patterson and the team were inconsistent. The second-year kicker had missed four of his first 18 field-goal attempts. A pair of those misses happened in a Week 10 matchup against the Kansas City Chiefs. The Jaguars lost 27–17 and dropped to a 3–7 record. The season seemed lost.

Then Patterson began to improve. In the final seven games of the year, he hit 16 of his 17 field-goal tries. He even kicked a late game-tying field goal in a thrilling comeback win over the Dallas Cowboys in overtime.

Jacksonville followed Patterson's lead. The team won six of its last seven games. With a 9–8 record, the Jaguars clinched not only

Kicker Riley Patterson, *right*, joined the Jaguars in 2022.

a playoff spot but an AFC South Division title. One week later, they were battling the Chargers in Jacksonville.

ANOTHER NAIL-BITER

Many of the Jaguars' games late in the season were comeback wins. The Jaguars took that to extremes by falling behind Los Angeles 27–0 in the first half of their playoff opener. But then Lawrence led Jacksonville to a stirring comeback. The offense took the field with 3:09 left. After driving 61 yards, the Jaguars had set up Patterson for a chance at glory.

Patterson trotted out to try and be the hero. Holder Logan Cooke took the snap and spotted the ball at the 26-yard line.

Patterson, *left*, celebrates with a teammate after kicking a 36-yard field goal against the Chargers.

Jacksonville outside linebacker Shaquille Quarterman waves the team's flag after beating the Chargers.

HISTORIC COMEBACK

The Jaguars' comeback against Los Angeles was the third largest in NFL playoff history. The Indianapolis Colts rallied from 28 points behind against Kansas City in a 2013 wild-card game. The Buffalo Bills battled back from 32 points down to beat the Houston Oilers in the 1992 wild-card round.

Patterson blasted the ball, then watched it slowly tail toward the right upright. Though twisting, the ball stayed just inside the post, and the Jaguars had an incredible 31–30 victory. "You dream of stuff like this as a kicker," Patterson later said. Jacksonville's championship dream was still alive.

"YOU DREAM OF STUFF LIKE THIS AS A KICKER."

—RILEY PATTERSON

NFL TEAMS MAP

NFC EAST

 DALLAS COWBOYS

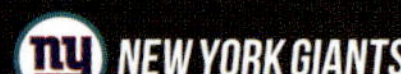 NEW YORK GIANTS

 PHILADELPHIA EAGLES

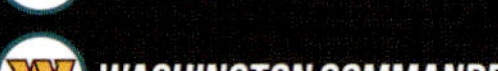 WASHINGTON COMMANDERS

NFC WEST

 ARIZONA CARDINALS

 LOS ANGELES RAMS

 SAN FRANCISCO 49ERS

 SEATTLE SEAHAWKS

NFC NORTH

 CHICAGO BEARS

 DETROIT LIONS

 GREEN BAY PACKERS

 MINNESOTA VIKINGS

NFC SOUTH

 ATLANTA FALCONS

 CAROLINA PANTHERS

 NEW ORLEANS SAINTS

 TAMPA BAY BUCCANEERS

AFC

AFC EAST

- BUFFALO BILLS
- MIAMI DOLPHINS
- NEW ENGLAND PATRIOTS
- NEW YORK JETS

AFC WEST

- DENVER BRONCOS
- KANSAS CITY CHIEFS
- LAS VEGAS RAIDERS
- LOS ANGELES CHARGERS

AFC NORTH

- BALTIMORE RAVENS
- CINCINNATI BENGALS
- CLEVELAND BROWNS
- PITTSBURGH STEELERS

AFC SOUTH

- HOUSTON TEXANS
- INDIANAPOLIS COLTS
-  JACKSONVILLE JAGUARS
- TENNESSEE TITANS

Wayne Weaver was instrumental in bringing the NFL to Jacksonville.

CHAPTER 2

JACKSONVILLE ARRIVES

In 1991, the NFL made a major announcement. For the first time in nearly two decades, the league was planning to add two new teams. Any new city wanting a team would have to submit a bid by 1992.

Jacksonville had a head start. In 1989, a group called Touchdown Jacksonville was formed in hopes of bringing an NFL team to the northeast Florida city. Jacksonville had a long history with the sport. Professional football was first played there in the 1920s. In the 1970s, Jacksonville had a team in the World Football League, which was a short-lived challenger to the NFL. A decade later, another Jacksonville team played in the United States Football League. But the league suspended play in 1986. Meanwhile, during

the 1970s and 1980s, multiple NFL teams threatened to move to Jacksonville. But none ever followed through.

Despite Jacksonville's history, the city was an underdog to receive one of the NFL's new teams. Charlotte was a fast-growing metropolis and seemed guaranteed a team. St. Louis and Baltimore had both lost NFL franchises in the 1980s and were thought to be preferred to Jacksonville. And all three were larger cities than Jacksonville. To promote Jacksonville, city officials produced a

The Gator Bowl, also known as Jacksonville Municipal Stadium, was upgraded to help the city get an NFL team.

video touting the city. It was narrated by celebrated actor James Earl Jones. Jacksonville's potential owner, Wayne Weaver, also gave a passionate speech at an NFL owners' meeting about his underdog city.

In October 1993, the NFL granted Charlotte a new team that would become the Carolina Panthers. The other cities had to wait a month as the NFL delayed its decision. Weaver was sure the NFL wanted St. Louis and thought the wait was just a tactic for the

Weaver's wife Delores, *left*, celebrates the announcement of Jacksonville as the NFL's 30th team in November 1993.

Missouri city to get its bid straightened out. But in a shocking move, on November 30, 1993, the owners voted 26–2 to place a team in Jacksonville.

FORMING THE JAGUARS

Weaver wanted his team to be ready to compete. In February 1994, 18 months before the team's first game, he hired Tom Coughlin as head coach. Coughlin also performed the duties of a general manager. He was a stern coach who wanted everyone to play by his rules. He was famous for setting clocks 15 minutes ahead to make sure none of his players

FINDING A NICKNAME

Like many NFL teams, Jacksonville held a contest to pick its nickname. The Jaguars name beat out Sharks and Stingrays in the final vote. At the time of the contest, the Jacksonville Zoo housed the oldest jaguar in North America.

Tom Coughlin, *in black*, had never been a head coach in the NFL before the Jaguars hired him in 1994.

were late. For Weaver, hiring Coughlin signaled that the Jaguars would be a serious team.

Coughlin had full control over player signings and draft picks. His first job was to oversee Jacksonville's expansion draft in February 1995. Each existing NFL team had to make some of its players available for the Jaguars to select, allowing the team to choose its first 31 players. Jacksonville's most notable pick was veteran quarterback Steve Beuerlein, who had been a starter for the Los Angeles Raiders, Phoenix Cardinals, and Dallas Cowboys.

At the regular NFL Draft two months later, Coughlin selected tough tackle Tony Boselli and running back James Stewart in the first round. While Stewart became a solid player, Boselli proved to be a cornerstone in the team's early years. Coughlin also made an unusual move when he signed wide receiver Jimmy Smith, who had not played in the NFL for two years. The 26-year-old receiver soon

Receiver Jimmy Smith (82) played for the Jaguars until 2005 and caught 862 passes for more than 12,000 yards and 67 touchdowns.

became a starter on his way to establishing several Jaguars career receiving records.

FRESH START

The Jaguars debuted on September 3, 1995, with a 10–3 loss to the Houston Oilers. Three more losses followed. While Beuerlein started the team's first two games and threw Jacksonville's first touchdown pass in a loss to the Cincinnati Bengals in Week 2, his hold on the starting job soon slipped.

Before the season, Coughlin had traded for young quarterback Mark Brunell to back up Beuerlein. Brunell had not been a prized prospect coming out of the University of Washington in 1993. At 6 feet, 1 inch tall, he was slightly shorter than the average NFL quarterback. Brunell was also left-handed, a rarity at the

Jacksonville offensive lineman Brian DeMarco celebrates the team's first-ever victory, a 17–16 win over the Houston Oilers on October 1, 1995.

position. And he'd spent his first two seasons backing up future Hall of Famer Brett Favre on the Green Bay Packers. Brunell rarely saw the field. So, when the Jaguars traded for him before the 1995 season, few fans even noticed.

Yet by Week 3, Brunell was elevated to the starting role. Though both quarterbacks ended up starting games as the season went on, Brunell's ability to scramble and to thrive under pressure stood out. With the Jaguars trailing in Week 5, Brunell came in to lead a fourth-quarter comeback to give Jacksonville its first win. He also started the other three Jacksonville wins in a 4–12 season.

Behind Brunell, the Jaguars appeared to have a quarterback they could count on in 1996. A bigger question was about coaching. Many Jacksonville players blamed Coughlin for the team's losses. They thought the coach's rules were too strict and practices too grueling.

Coughlin earned the nickname "Tom the Tyrant." He fined players for wearing the wrong-colored socks or the wrong type of tie on road trips. Many players felt Coughlin treated them as high school or college students instead of professional athletes. By nine games into the 1996 season, the Jaguars were a lowly 3–6 and Coughlin saw he was losing touch with his players. Entering the team's Week 10 bye, Coughlin decided to loosen the rules and make practices less brutal. Suddenly, the Jaguars took off.

Jacksonville had plenty of talent. Brunell had become one of the league's most exciting quarterbacks. Though he threw a fair number of interceptions, his aggressive style led to big plays. And as a runner, Brunell rarely went out of bounds or slid. He sometimes hurdled oncoming defenders. Other times he simply took hits to gain extra yards.

Along the way, the young quarterback built a strong connection with Smith and free agent receiver Keenan McCardell. Like Brunell, both had arrived in Jacksonville as unwanted players. Smith was a second-round draft pick of the Dallas Cowboys in 1992. In his first two years, he was a part of two Super Bowl championship teams. But he rarely played.

Quarterback Mark Brunell threw for a Jaguars-record 25,698 yards in nine seasons.

For four seasons, receiver Keenan McCardell (8) caught at least 80 passes each year while playing for the Jaguars.

Smith appeared in seven games as a rookie without catching a pass. Before the 1993 season, he suffered from appendicitis during training camp and required surgery. He watched the entire season from the sideline, and then Dallas cut him in 1994. After spending a year out of football, Smith signed with the Jaguars. Though he became the first Jaguars player to ever touch the football in a game when he returned the team's first kickoff, he ended the season with only 22 catches.

McCardell was a 12th-round pick by Washington in 1991 but never played for the team. He spent three years with the Cleveland Browns and broke out with 56 catches in 1995. That performance came just in time, as the 26-year-old was a free agent. He signed

with Jacksonville in the offseason, and he quickly formed a dangerous passing unit with Smith and Brunell.

Meanwhile, Boselli emerged as one of the best left tackles in football. He blocked for two powerful running backs in Stewart and Natrone Means. Linebackers Kevin Hardy and Eddie Robinson anchored the defense.

The team's abilities showed in a Week 11 matchup against the Baltimore Ravens as Jacksonville rallied to win 30–27. Though the Jaguars lost big the next weekend, they went on to win

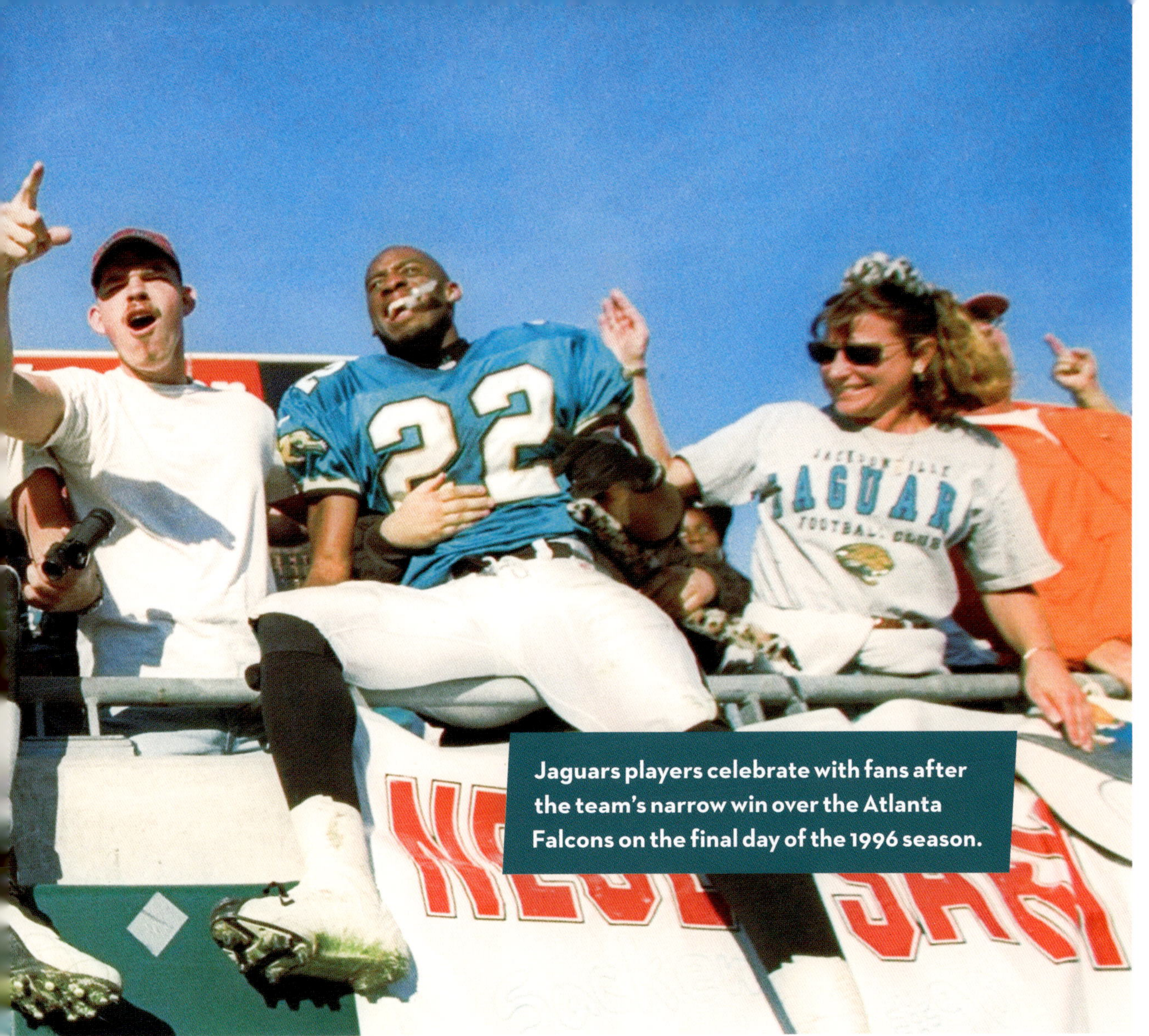

Jaguars players celebrate with fans after the team's narrow win over the Atlanta Falcons on the final day of the 1996 season.

their next four games, all by close margins. That set up a big regular-season finale against the Atlanta Falcons, with a playoff berth on the line for Jacksonville.

The Jaguars and Falcons fought down to the wire. With most of their points coming from four field goals by kicker Mike Hollis, Jacksonville held a 19–17 lead late in the fourth quarter. But Atlanta drove to put its kicker, Morten Andersen, in position to win the game. Andersen's 30-yard kick went wide, and the Jaguars clinched their first playoff berth.

Wide receiver Jimmy Smith grabbed 862 catches and 67 touchdown passes in 11 years with Jacksonville.

CHAPTER 3

MAKING A NAME

JACKSONVILLE ENTERED THE 1996 POSTSEASON AS AN UNDERDOG. THE Jaguars opened the playoffs in Buffalo to play the Bills, who had never lost a playoff game at their Rich Stadium. Many experts thought the Jaguars would quickly be eliminated. With no pressure on them, the Jaguars were carefree. "We had nothing to lose," wide receiver Keenan McCardell said. "Let's just go out and play loose and see what happens."

"WE HAD NOTHING TO LOSE. LET'S JUST GO OUT AND PLAY LOOSE AND SEE WHAT HAPPENS."

—KEENAN MCCARDELL

In a hard-fought game, Mark Brunell threw an interception that was returned for a touchdown in the fourth quarter to put the Bills ahead 27–20. But the quarterback regrouped. On Jacksonville's next drive, Brunell threw a 1-yard touchdown pass to Jimmy Smith to tie the game. After a Bills fumble, Mike Hollis kicked a 45-yard field goal that banked in off the right upright. The Jaguars claimed a 30–27 victory.

TONY BOSELLI

At 6 feet, 7 inches tall and 324 pounds, offensive tackle Tony Boselli engulfed defenders. He first made a name for himself in Jacksonville's 30–27 playoff win over the Buffalo Bills in January 1996. During that game, Boselli stuffed Bills star Bruce Smith, the NFL's all-time leader in sacks. Boselli was named to the NFL's team of the 1990s, despite playing only half the decade. In 2022, he was the first Jaguar ever inducted into the Pro Football Hall of Fame.

Jacksonville visited Denver next to face the powerful Broncos. Before the game, a Denver sportswriter dismissed the Jaguars as a terrible team. Again, most experts favored Jacksonville's competition. Early in the matchup, that prediction looked correct as the Broncos raced to a 12–0 lead.

Then the Jaguars came roaring back. By halftime, they led 13–12. Brunell opened the third quarter with a 31-yard touchdown pass to McCardell. Hollis added the extra point and then another field goal. The Broncos responded with a touchdown and two-point conversion to make the score 23–20 Jacksonville.

Then Brunell hit Smith on a 16-yard touchdown strike late in the fourth quarter.

Quarterback Mark Brunell looks to pass during a playoff game against the Denver Broncos in January 1997.

Despite giving up a late touchdown, the Jaguars held on for another 30–27 win. After the game, the victorious Jaguars returned to Jacksonville and were greeted by 40,000 fans at their Municipal Stadium. The crowd had watched the game on the stadium's video board and stayed to welcome the players home.

END OF THE RUN

After the victory in Denver, Jacksonville went back on the road to face the New England Patriots. On a frigid afternoon in Foxboro, Massachusetts, Jacksonville committed several mistakes. New England took advantage and led 13–3 at halftime.

Hollis kicked a third-quarter field goal, bringing Jacksonville within a touchdown of the Patriots. Early in the fourth quarter, the Jaguars drove deep into New England territory. On second-and-goal from the New England 5, Brunell fired a pass

Defensive end Tony Brackens (90) had a team-record 55 sacks between 1996 and 2003.

over the middle of the field. However, New England defensive back Willie Clay intercepted it in the end zone with 13:11 left. On the first play of their next drive, James Stewart was stripped of the ball by New England linebacker Chris Slade. Patriots cornerback Otis Smith recovered the fumble and raced 45 yards for a touchdown, sealing a 20–6 defeat for the Jaguars.

The stinging loss left the Jaguars one step short of a surprising Super Bowl bid. But Jacksonville had certainly proved itself as a tough team with devoted fans. The Jaguars were ready for the 1997 season.

CONTENDERS

The Jaguars had shown that they could be a dangerous team in 1996, especially on offense. Brunell led the NFL in passing that season. McCardell had a team-high 85 catches for 1,129 yards.

Jimmy Smith led the Jaguars with 1,243 receiving yards and seven touchdowns on 83 receptions.

Jacksonville's momentum carried into a 5-2 start in 1997. On October 26, the team traveled to Pittsburgh for a divisional showdown against the Steelers. The Jaguars had already beaten the Steelers earlier in the season. But that afternoon, Jacksonville tossed away two leads and lost in overtime.

It was only the middle of the season, but the loss was a costly one. Both the Jaguars and Steelers finished with 11-5 records. That meant tiebreakers were needed to determine the AFC Central champion. Since both teams were tied in division record, conference record, and record in similar games, the fifth tiebreaker, net-division points, would determine the winner. The Steelers had the edge by outscoring the other three divisional opponents by

The Jaguars selected linebacker Kevin Hardy with the second overall pick in the 1996 NFL Draft.

more points than Jacksonville had during the year. Pittsburgh won the division.

Since the Jaguars lost the tiebreaker, they had to play in the wild-card round of the playoffs. Pittsburgh got a bye to the second weekend of the postseason. Jacksonville faced off against the Broncos, who wanted revenge against the Jaguars for ending their 1996 postseason. Jacksonville struggled in the rematch. The Broncos rushed for 310 yards and five touchdowns in a 42–17 rout. Jacksonville's season was over.

Running back Fred Taylor finished third in Rookie of the Year voting after the 1998 regular season.

The Jaguars had already exceeded most people's expectations for the first three years of an expansion team. In 1998, they drafted a new offensive weapon. Running back Fred Taylor had grown up in Pahokee, Florida. Taylor then starred at the University of Florida in Gainesville, just 72 miles (116 km) from Jacksonville. Twice in his college career, he had played in Jacksonville Municipal Stadium.

Cornerback Fernando Bryant, *right*, intercepts a pass against the Kansas City Chiefs during the 1999 preseason.

The Jaguars' home hosted the annual game between Florida and rival Georgia.

Taylor was a former sprinter for his high school track team. He still had blazing speed when he joined the NFL. During his rookie year, he rushed for 1,223 yards and 14 touchdowns as the Jaguars went 11–5. That was good enough for a division title. By reaching the playoffs, the Jaguars had made history. No NFL expansion team had ever competed in the postseason three times in its first four years.

Taylor dominated with 162 rushing yards and a touchdown in a 25–10 wild-card win over the Patriots. But in the divisional round, the New York Jets held him out of the end zone. On defense, Jacksonville couldn't stop New York. The Jets totaled more than 400 offensive yards and won 34–24.

ALL IN

After two years of poor defense in the postseason, Jaguars coach Tom Coughlin made more changes in 1999. He drafted cornerback Fernando Bryant in the first round. Then he shored up the defense

Taylor bursts past a Miami Dolphins defender during a playoff game on January 15, 2000.

by adding veteran defensive tackle Gary Walker and safety Carnell Lake.

The additions made a huge difference. While the offense continued its high-level play, Jacksonville stuffed opponents. The Jaguars allowed the fewest points in the league and finished 14–2. Bryant picked off two passes and led the team with three fumble recoveries. Walker added 10 sacks, and defensive end Tony Brackens led the team with 12.

In the 1999 divisional playoff round, the Miami Dolphins traveled up the coast to face Jacksonville. Legendary quarterback Dan Marino led Miami. The 17-year veteran had broken numerous passing records in his career.

The Jaguars were aggressive, leading 10–0 with four minutes left in the first quarter. Backed up to their own 10-yard line, Taylor took Brunell's handoff and bounced out to the right side. He skipped over one potential tackler at the line of scrimmage, then slipped past two more with clever jukes. From there, Taylor flew past Miami defensive back Brock Marion and raced 90 yards down the sideline. It was the longest run in NFL postseason history.

Tackle Gary Walker sacks Miami quarterback Dan Marino.

Jacksonville was just getting warmed up. After the next kickoff, Miami started at its own 26. On the first play, Brackens sprinted around a Dolphins offensive tackle, stripped the ball from Marino, and quickly fell on it. As 75,000 fans screamed, no one heard that the whistle never blew. The Dolphins never touched Brackens, meaning the play was still live. Even Brackens wasn't sure as he got up and started a celebratory dance. A handful of teammates surrounded the defensive end and shouted for him to run toward the end zone. By the time the Dolphins realized what was happening, Brackens had crossed the goal line. With two touchdowns in 25 seconds, Jacksonville increased its lead to 23–0.

The Jaguars never let up. Taylor caught a 39-yard touchdown pass from Brunell in the second quarter. Less than three minutes later, Stewart rushed in from 25 yards. Hollis booted a field goal, making the score 41–0. The Dolphins broke the shutout on a touchdown pass with one second left in the first half, but the game was essentially over. Jacksonville's starters barely played in the second half in what became a 62–7 demolition. It was both the highest scoring playoff game and the biggest postseason blowout in the league since the Chicago Bears beat Washington 73–0 in the 1940 NFL Championship Game.

The Jaguars' historic win set up a second AFC title game against their division rival Tennessee Titans. Though Jacksonville had won the AFC Central, its only two losses that year were delivered by the Titans. In the championship game, Jacksonville took a 14–10 lead into halftime. But in the third quarter, an explosive two-play sequence would decide the game.

Tennessee took a 17–14 lead with 9:27 left in the third. Just over four minutes later, Brunell was sacked in the end zone for a safety. Trailing 19–14, the Jaguars then had to kick the ball away to the Titans. Tennessee receiver Derrick Mason caught the ball at his own 20 and sprinted 80 yards for a touchdown. The Jaguars never recovered, falling 33–14. For the second time in the Jaguars' short history, they came up one step short of the Super Bowl.

Jacksonville tight end Kyle Brady catches a touchdown pass in the AFC Championship Game against the Tennessee Titans on January 23, 2000.

Offensive tackle Tony Boselli reached the Pro Bowl five times while playing for the Jacksonville Jaguars.

CHAPTER 4

NEW DIRECTIONS

In the early 1990s, the NFL had put in a salary cap to prevent teams from outspending one another. The salary cap ensured more teams would be competitive each season, but it also made it harder for good teams to stay together for a long time. That proved to be the case in Jacksonville. As the Jaguars improved through the late part of the decade, they had spent big on players. By the end of the 1999 season, Jacksonville was forced to cut back.

Several veteran players, including original running back James Stewart, were let go before the 2000 season. Struggling to replace these players, the Jaguars finished 7–9. When the team didn't improve much over the next few seasons, more veterans left.

Among the biggest losses was Tony Boselli. The stellar left tackle had played only three games in 2001 as Jacksonville finished 6–10. Boselli needed surgery to fix an injured shoulder. When it didn't heal properly, the Jaguars made him available for the newest expansion team, the Houston Texans. Houston selected Boselli with its first pick, but the Hall of Fame tackle never played for the Texans. He officially retired a year later, having spent his entire seven-season career with the Jaguars.

Wide receiver Keenan McCardell also departed at the end of the 2001 season. He signed a big contract with the Tampa Bay Buccaneers. McCardell caught two touchdown passes in a Super Bowl victory during his first season with Tampa Bay. Meanwhile, the Jaguars continued to slide, finishing the 2002 season just 6–10.

A NEW ERA

Looking for a change, the Jaguars fired Tom Coughlin and brought in Panthers defensive coordinator Jack Del Rio to replace him. One of Del Rio's first big tasks was finding a long-term solution at quarterback. Brunell was 32 at the end of the 2002 season. Years of scrambling and taking big hits had slowed him down. So, in 2003, the Jaguars drafted Marshall University star quarterback Byron Leftwich in the

Tom Coughlin had a 68–60 record in his eight seasons with the Jaguars.

Quarterback Byron Leftwich (7) looks to pass during a game against the Minnesota Vikings in 2004.

first round. Del Rio hoped Leftwich would learn under Brunell to lead the team.

The learning phase didn't last long. After three losses to start the season, Leftwich took over as the starter, leading the team to a 5–11 record. The offense still leaned on Smith and Fred Taylor, who remained one of the best backs in the NFL when he was healthy. Together that trio led the Jaguars back to a winning record in 2004.

Unfortunately, Taylor frequently missed time with injuries. In 2005, as the Jaguars put together a 12–4 season and their first playoff berth in six years, Taylor played only 11 games. By that point, the Jacksonville media had dubbed him "Fragile Fred."

PLAYOFF DISAPPOINTMENT

Leftwich was trying to pull off a miracle. The Jaguars trailed the New England Patriots 28–3 early in the fourth quarter of their wild-card matchup after the 2005 season. The young quarterback, still struggling with a healing broken ankle that had forced him to miss the final month of the regular season, was facing third-and-two at the Patriots' 8-yard line. Leftwich dropped back to pass and was pressured by New England linebacker Willie McGinest. Forced backward, Leftwich was sacked for a 15-yard loss. On the next play, Jacksonville kicker Josh Scobee missed a field-goal attempt.

Defensive tackle Marcus Stroud, *right*, made the Pro Bowl three times in seven seasons with the Jaguars.

The powerhouse Patriots were relentless against the Jaguars. Leftwich was pounded all game. He suffered four sacks, fumbled once, and threw an interception. He was replaced partway through

Leftwich, *left*, is sacked by New England Patriots' Willie McGinest in a playoff matchup in January 2006.

the fourth quarter by backup David Garrard. Neither team scored another point, and New England won 28–3. Jacksonville's rebound season ended with a thud.

Leftwich was a towering quarterback with a big arm. But he struggled with inconsistency and injuries. In 2006, he sprained his ankle and missed the rest of the season. During the 2007 preseason, Garrard took over the starting job. By the time Week 1 rolled around, the highly touted Leftwich had been cut from the team.

Garrard, like Brunell, wasn't a top prospect. But the former fourth-round pick was a steady leader at quarterback. In 2007, he threw 18 touchdown passes and only three interceptions. His stellar play helped guide the team back to the playoffs for the second time in three years.

The quarterback was not the team's only talent. Taylor rushed for more than 1,200 yards. In 2006, he was joined in the backfield by second-round pick Maurice Jones-Drew. Though standing only 5 feet, 7 inches tall, the former University of California Los Angeles (UCLA) running back could muscle through would-be tacklers with his powerful legs. Jones-Drew's quick feet let him dance around defenders. The second-year player added 768 yards and a team-high nine rushing touchdowns as the Jaguars boasted the top rushing attack in the AFC.

Cornerback Rashean Mathis had two interceptions, including one that he returned 63 yards for a touchdown, during a wild-card game in January 2008.

ON THE MOVE

When the Houston Texans became part of the NFL in 2002, the league realigned its divisions. The Jaguars were moved from the AFC Central to the AFC South. There, they joined Houston along with the Tennessee Titans and Indianapolis Colts.

The Jaguars line up against the Indianapolis Colts during a game in 2005.

After finishing second in the AFC South, the Jaguars earned a wild-card playoff spot and traveled to Pittsburgh to take on the Steelers. Jones-Drew shone in the national spotlight. After Pittsburgh scored a touchdown on its opening drive, Jones-Drew responded by returning the next kickoff 96 yards to the Steelers' 1-yard line. Taylor scored on the next play to tie the game.

In the second quarter, Jacksonville led 14–7 when Jones-Drew caught a swing pass from Garrard and raced 43 yards down the sideline for a touchdown. He then dashed around the left tackle for a 10-yard touchdown, raising the Jaguars' lead to 28–10.

Early in the fourth quarter, the Steelers fought back. Pittsburgh scored three times in just over eight minutes. Though they failed on a pair of two-point conversions, the Steelers led 29–28 with 6:21 left.

Jacksonville kicker Josh Scobee (10) kicks a field goal in the playoff game against the Pittsburgh Steelers in January 2008.

The score had not changed when the Jaguars took over at their own 49 with 2:38 to play. Three plays later, Jacksonville faced fourth-and-two at the Pittsburgh 43. Garrard, who had rushed for only 185 yards all season, burst through the middle on a quarterback draw play. By the time he was dragged down, the quarterback had gained 32 yards.

Quarterback David Garrard (9) is hit by New England defensive tackle Ty Warren in a divisional-round game on January 12, 2008.

Four plays later, Scobee booted the go-ahead field goal with 40 seconds left, giving Jacksonville the lead. On the next drive, the Jaguars' defense sealed the win by forcing a fumble from Pittsburgh quarterback Ben Roethlisberger.

That nail-biting 31–29 victory earned the Jaguars another trip to New England to face the undefeated Patriots in the divisional round. The teams were tied 14–14 at halftime. But the Patriots held Jones-Drew to just 19 yards on the ground. Meanwhile, Jacksonville's defense couldn't contain New England's legendary quarterback, Tom Brady. The superstar completed 26 of 28 passes for 262 yards and three touchdowns. New England ran away with a 31–20 win.

EMPTY SEATS

The Jaguars couldn't keep their playoff momentum going after the 2007 season. The team slipped to 5–11 the next year. But the team had bigger problems in the stands.

Jacksonville had long played in one of the NFL's largest stadiums. When Jacksonville Municipal Stadium opened in 1995, it held 73,000 fans. It expanded to 76,877 in 2003. However, within two years the team had many empty seats at each game. At the time, NFL games that weren't sold out could not be seen on local television. To combat this, the Jaguars started putting large tarps over sections of seats to lower the number of seats they had to sell.

Even with a reduced capacity, the Jaguars still couldn't fill their stadium. A nationwide financial crisis in the late 2000s hit Florida especially hard. Many fans could no longer afford tickets even though the Jaguars had some of the lowest prices in the league. In 2008 alone, the Jaguars lost 17,000 season-ticket holders.

Jacksonville's home stadium, now known as EverBank Stadium, was outfitted with two new screens in 2014. Each was 60 feet (18.3 m) high and 362 feet (110.3 m) long.

Running back Maurice Jones-Drew stiff-arms a defender from the Cincinnati Bengals during a game in 2011.

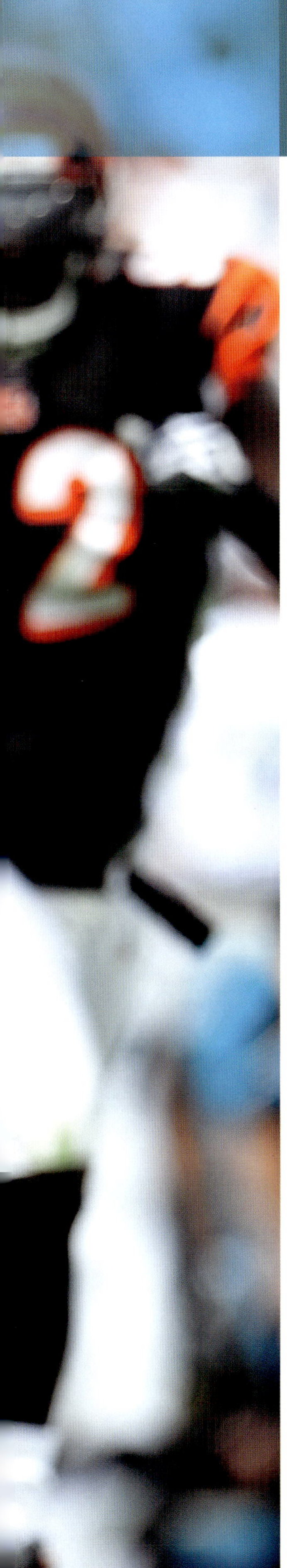

CHAPTER 5

BITING BACK

MAURICE JONES-DREW COMMANDED THE 2011 SEASON. The 26-year-old back rushed for an NFL-best 1,606 yards. Jones-Drew also led the league with 386 touches, which included rushing attempts and catches. His 43 receptions were one shy of the Jaguars' team lead. Jones-Drew rushed for eight touchdowns and caught three more through the air.

Unfortunately for Jacksonville, their star back's efforts could not carry the team. Jones-Drew's 1,980 total yards accounted for nearly half of the team's total offense. The Jaguars finished 5–11. Jack Del Rio was fired with five games left in Jacksonville's fourth straight nonwinning season. There would be bigger changes to the team beyond a new head coach.

Shad Khan, *right*, is introduced by NFL commissioner Roger Goodell after buying the Jaguars.

MAKING HISTORY

On December 14, 2011, Shad Khan officially purchased the Jaguars from Wayne Weaver for $770 million. Khan was born in Pakistan and immigrated to the United States. He became the first owner of color in the NFL. Khan cut a striking figure with his bold, curlicue mustache and stylish hair. He had plenty of work to do to return the team to success on the field.

When Khan took over, the Jaguars were a mess. Years of poor drafting had left the team short on talent. In 2012, the first year of Khan's ownership, Jacksonville drafted highly touted receiver Justin Blackmon. The talented pass-catcher was out of the league after just two partial seasons due to his problems with substance use. Between 2012 and 2016, the Jaguars finished with a record of 17–63. Two head coaches were hired and fired in that span. A third coach was hired during the 2016 season.

SACKSONVILLE

Though the Jaguars struggled, the foundations of a strong defensive unit were coming together. Between 2014 and 2017, the Jaguars drafted pass rushers Yannick Ngakoue and Dante Fowler, pairing them with free agent Malik Jackson. Linebacker Myles Jack was a second-round pick in 2016. He joined 2014 pick Telvin Smith and free agent pickup Paul Posluszny to form a stout tackling unit. Ultra-confident cornerback Jalen Ramsey had six interceptions in that time span, while fellow corner A. J. Bouye and safeties Barry Church and Tashaun Gipson had four each.

In the team's first full year under head coach Doug Marrone, the Jaguars shocked the NFL by finishing 10–6. The defense pressured quarterbacks so much that the team earned the nickname "Sacksonville." That tough play helped overcome a mediocre offense led by erratic third-year quarterback Blake Bortles and rookie

Quarterback Blake Bortles set team records of 4,428 passing yards and 35 touchdowns during the 2015 season.

runner Leonard Fournette. Of the team's 10 wins, seven came while holding its opponents to seven points or less.

After the 2017 season, the Jaguars reached the playoffs for the first time in a decade. They then shut down the Buffalo Bills 10–3 in the wild-card round. When the defense had a rare bad day in the divisional round against the Pittsburgh Steelers, the offense picked up the slack. Fournette rushed for 109 yards and three touchdowns in a 45–42 shootout win.

Cornerback Jalen Ramsey was an All-Pro performer in 2017.

For the fifth time in Jaguars history, the team squared off against the New England Patriots in the postseason. Since 2000, the Jaguars reached the playoffs only three times. During that time, the Patriots had played in seven Super Bowls,

Rookie running back Leonard Fournette rushed for 1,040 yards and nine touchdowns during the 2017 season.

Jacksonville tackle Marcell Dareus (99) takes down New England quarterback Tom Brady in the AFC title game on January 21, 2018.

winning five. They were led by quarterback Tom Brady, one of the most feared postseason players in the NFL.

A CLOSE CALL

Despite the historic mismatch, the Jaguars came out strong. Bortles threw a touchdown pass and Fournette ran for another to put the Jaguars up 14–3. New England finally reached the end zone with 55 seconds left in the first half. In the third quarter, Jacksonville kicker Josh Lambo responded with a field goal. He fired off another early in the fourth quarter, giving the Jaguars a 20–10 lead.

A little more than a minute into the final quarter, the Patriots tried a trick play in which receiver Danny Amendola threw a pass to

Linebacker Myles Jack (44) shows his frustration after officials ruled him down following his fourth-quarter fumble recovery against New England.

running back Dion Lewis. After Lewis gained 20 yards, Jack snuck in from behind and stripped the ball away, recovering it as he fell to the ground. The whistle blew just as Jack got up and ran the other way. He continued down a clear path to the end zone. No defender had touched him, but the officials thought he was down. The play was dead. The score remained 20-10 Jacksonville.

Jacksonville failed to move the ball on its next drive. Given a second chance, Brady threw a touchdown pass to Amendola. He then sent another touchdown strike to Amendola with 2:56 left.

The Patriots took a 24–20 lead. Jacksonville reached New England's 43 with 1:47 to go. But Bortles threw an incomplete pass on fourth-and-15, ending Jacksonville's upset bid.

COMING APART

For the third time, the Jaguars finished one step short of the Super Bowl. With a promising defense and rookie star Fournette, Jacksonville fans hoped better days lay ahead. However, things soon started to unravel.

Behind the scenes, the 2017 Jaguars were a dysfunctional team. Prior to the season, original coach Tom Coughlin had returned as the Jaguars' president. He soon dismantled the team. By the end of the 2019 season, stars such as Fowler and Ramsey had been traded. Smith and Posluszny had both retired. Many other players were simply cut.

Jaguars tight end James O'Shaughnessy racked up 149 receiving yards in 2017.

With so much talent heading out the door, Jacksonville fell fast. The team had won five games in 2018. Two years later the Jaguars finished 1–15. Needing a change, Jacksonville added a new quarterback and coach. In the 2021 NFL Draft, the Jaguars selected Clemson's highly touted Trevor Lawrence. The team also brought on Urban Meyer, who had coached both Florida and Ohio State to college national championships. While Lawrence showed promise as a rookie, Meyer turned out to be a disaster. He lasted only 13 games into a 3–13 season before being fired. In that short time, Meyer was fined by the NFL for breaking practice rules and accused by several players of abusive behavior. The biggest charge came from Lambo, who said Meyer kicked him during a practice.

Trevor Lawrence completed 387 passes in 2022.

THE COMEBACK CATS

In 2022, the Jaguars hired Super Bowl–winning coach Doug Pederson. With Lawrence playing inconsistently, Jacksonville started the year just 3–7. In Week 12, the Jaguars hosted Baltimore. Down 27–20, Lawrence threw a late touchdown pass to receiver Marvin Jones. The quarterback then hit wide receiver Zay Jones for a two-point conversion to win 28–27 over the Ravens.

Three weeks later, the Jaguars trailed the Dallas Cowboys 27–10 in the third quarter. But Jacksonville battled back. Lawrence tossed three touchdown passes. Kicker Riley Patterson booted a 48-yard field goal as time expired to force overtime. In the extra period, Jaguars defensive back Rayshawn Jenkins picked off a deflected pass and sprinted 52 yards for the winning touchdown.

The dramatic win pushed the Jaguars to 6–8. Following the game, receiver Christian Kirk said, "We're here to flip the script." And after two more wins, Jacksonville entered Week 17 needing a win to clinch a playoff spot. The Jaguars fell behind the Tennessee Titans 16–10 after three quarters. But Patterson kicked a 36-yard field goal early in the fourth. With 2:51 to play, linebacker Josh Hines-Allen scooped up a fumble from Tennessee quarterback Joshua Dobbs and raced 37 yards for the winning score. The thrilling victory sealed the AFC South title and a playoff bid for Jacksonville.

> ***"WE'RE HERE TO FLIP THE SCRIPT."***
>
> ***—CHRISTIAN KIRK***

After a slow start to the 2022 season, Lawrence transformed into an excellent player. The previous year he led the NFL with 17 interceptions. In 2022, he threw only eight and tossed

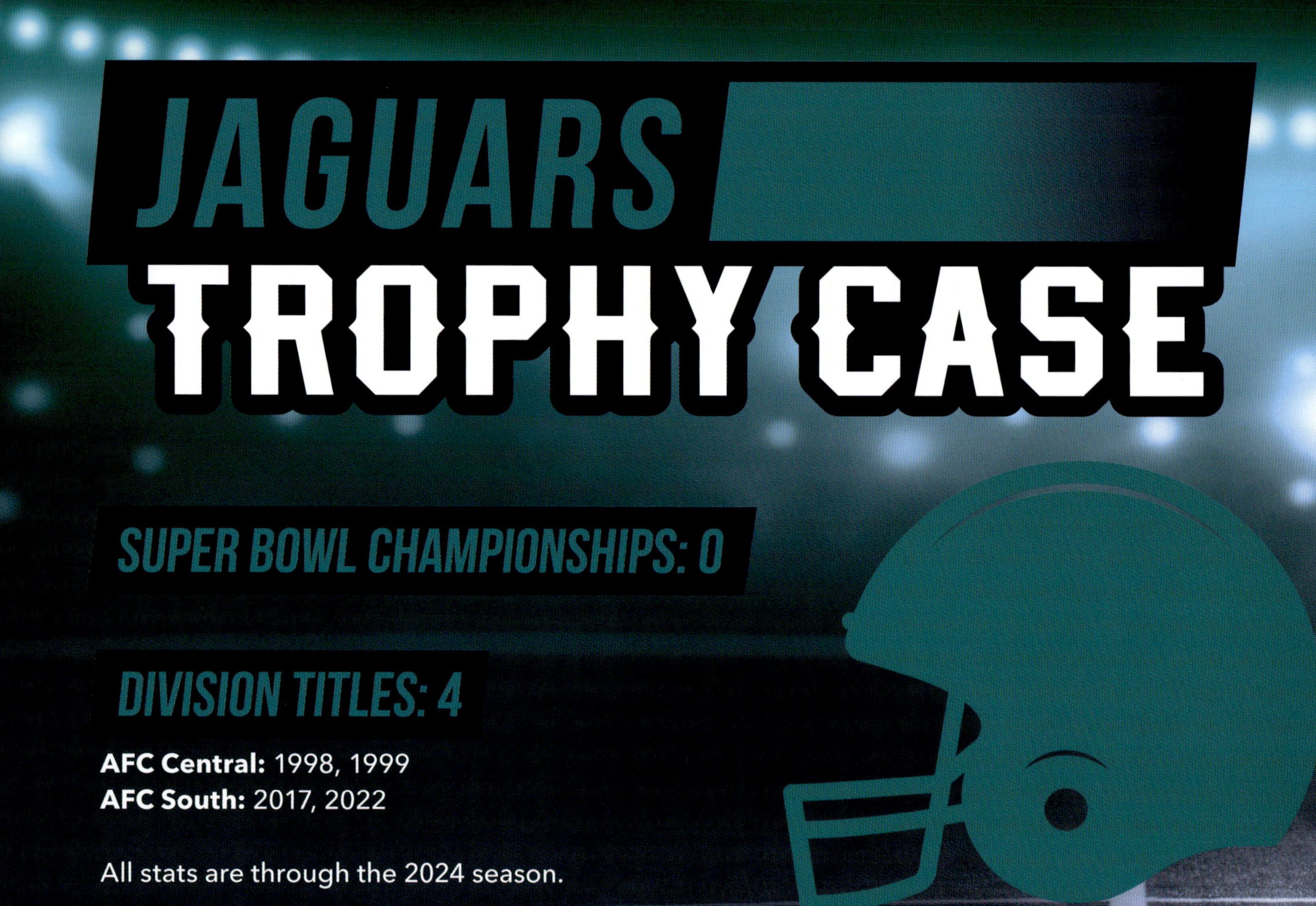

25 touchdown passes. But in the first half of the wild-card round game against the Los Angeles Chargers, the second-year quarterback misfired again. Lawrence threw four interceptions in six first-half drives while the Chargers built a 27–0 lead. Jaguars fans even booed their star quarterback.

Despite appearing discouraged, Lawrence refused to back down. He threw one touchdown pass with 24 seconds left before halftime. Lawrence was hungry for more and fired another touchdown pass in the third quarter. Then with 44 seconds left in the third quarter, he sent a 39-yard touchdown pass to Zay Jones.

Linebacker Josh Hines-Allen returns a fumble for a game-winning touchdown against the Titans in Week 18 of the 2022 season.

Defensive back Rayshawn Jenkins races for his game-winning touchdown against the Dallas Cowboys in 2022.

The Jaguars failed on the two-point conversion, but they shrank the Chargers' lead to 30–20.

With 5:25 left in the fourth, Lawrence threw his fourth touchdown pass, a 9-yarder to Kirk. Lawrence then ran the two-point conversion in himself. It was a two-point game.

The Jaguars got the ball back with 3:09 left at their own 21-yard line. Lawrence gained most of the early yards himself. In a series of four plays, he threw for 26 yards and ran for eight more. After Lawrence's old Clemson teammate Travis Etienne ran for 25 yards, Patterson kicked the game-winning field goal. The Jaguars walked off the field with an improbable victory.

Jacksonville's playoff run came to an end a week later at the hands of the NFL's newest dynasty. Despite battling hard, the Jaguars came up short against the eventual Super Bowl champion Kansas City Chiefs 27–20. Once again, the Jaguars didn't capitalize on their success. Though the team finished 9–8 again in 2023, that wasn't good enough to reach the playoffs. Jacksonville stumbled badly in 2024. Lawrence missed much of the season with injuries, and the team fell to 4–13. Head coach Doug Pederson was let go. Once again, the fans in Jacksonville felt like the team was starting over.

JACKSONVILLE IN LONDON

Starting in 2007, the NFL has played a few games in London, England, each season. Over the next few years, rumors flew that the league might move a team to London. As the Jaguars were struggling for attendance, they were viewed as a possible candidate. Instead, the Jaguars began playing one game per year in London in 2013, except for 2020. In 2023, Jacksonville began playing two games in London each year.

TIMELINE

Jacksonville is granted an expansion franchise by the NFL.
1993

The Jaguars upset the Buffalo Bills and the Denver Broncos to advance to the AFC title game but lose 20-6 to the New England Patriots on January 12.
1997

After drafting star running back Fred Taylor, the Jaguars win their first division title.
1998

Stars Keenan McCardell and Tony Boselli leave the team after Jacksonville finishes with a losing record for the second consecutive season.
2001

1994
Team owner Wayne Weaver hires Tom Coughlin as head coach.

1997
The Jaguars finish 11-5 but lose to the Broncos in the first round of the playoffs on December 27.

2000
The Jaguars finish the season 14-2 and then rout the Miami Dolphins 62-7 in the divisional round of the playoffs. They fall to the Tennessee Titans in the AFC title game on January 23.

2002
Tom Coughlin is fired as head coach.

2006
Under coach Jack Del Rio, the Jaguars finish 12-4 but lose 28-3 to the Patriots in the wild-card round on January 7.

2008
Jacksonville defeats the Pittsburgh Steelers in the wild-card round before losing to the Patriots in the divisional round on January 12.

2011
Shad Khan purchases the Jaguars for $770 million.

2018
The "Sacksonville" Jaguars reach the AFC title game but lose a 20-10 lead in the fourth quarter of a 24-20 loss to the Patriots on January 21.

2021
After finishing a league worst 1-15 in 2020, the Jaguars select quarterback Trevor Lawrence with the top pick in the NFL Draft.

2023
The Jaguars come back from 27-0 down in the wild-card round of the playoffs to defeat the Los Angeles Chargers 31-30 on January 14.

GLOSSARY

bye–when a team is allowed to skip a round in the playoffs due to its strong showing in the regular season.

contract–an agreement to play for a certain team.

draft–a system that allows teams to acquire new players coming into a league.

dynasty–a team that has an extended period of success, usually winning multiple championships in the process.

erratic–prone to making mistakes.

expansion draft–a special draft held to stock a new team using players from existing teams in the same league.

expansion team–a new team that is added to an existing league.

franchise–an entire sports organization.

free agent–a player who is not signed to a team.

general manager–an executive who runs a team and is responsible for finding and signing players.

postseason–another word for playoffs; the time after the end of the regular season when teams play to determine a champion.

rookie–a professional athlete in his or her first year of competition.

sack–a tackle of the quarterback behind the line of scrimmage before he can pass the ball.

safety–a score of two points for a team when its opponent is unable to advance the ball out of its own end zone.

tactic–a carefully planned action or strategy.

tiebreaker—a system designed to decide a winner between two teams with the same record.

two-point conversion—an option for teams that have scored a touchdown to try a running or passing play from the 2-yard line for two points, instead of kicking for one point.

underdog—the person or team that is not expected to win.

upright—one of the two vertical poles on a goalpost.

veteran—someone who has played for many years.

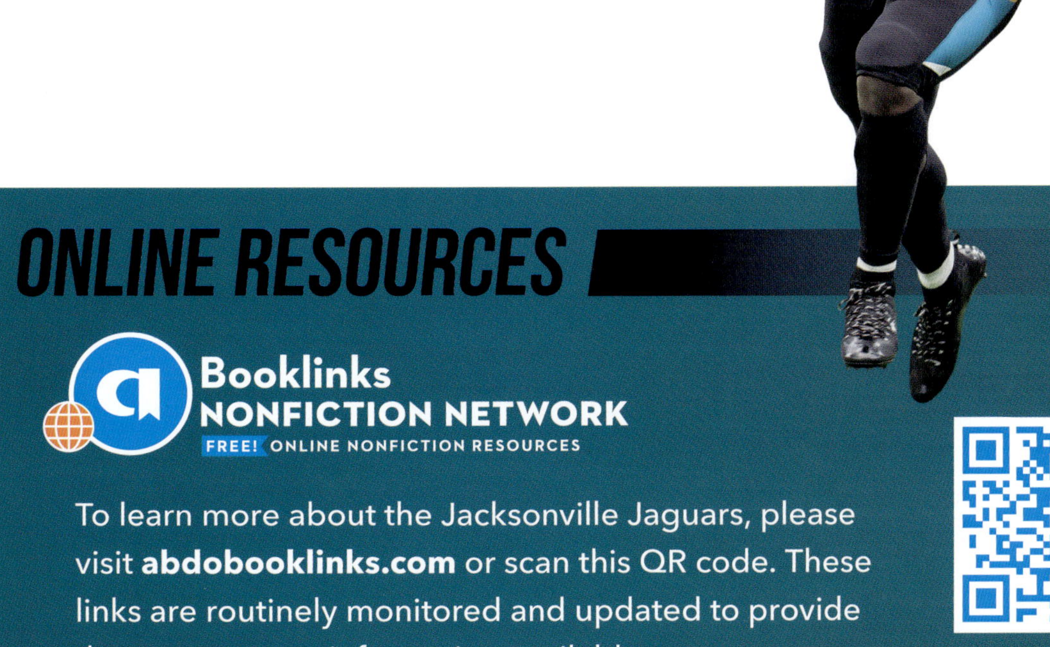

ONLINE RESOURCES

Booklinks
NONFICTION NETWORK
FREE! ONLINE NONFICTION RESOURCES

To learn more about the Jacksonville Jaguars, please visit **abdobooklinks.com** or scan this QR code. These links are routinely monitored and updated to provide the most current information available.

INDEX